Change Your Mind

57 WAYS TO UNLOCK YOUR CREATIVE SELF

ROD JUDKINS

hardie grant books

TO ZELDA, SCARLET AND LOUIS.

Change Your Mind

57 WAYS TO UNLOCK YOUR CREATIVE SELF

ROD JUDKINS

hardie grant books

Great artists, designers, musicians and writers are

...

ordinary

they
come
from
ordinary
**families,
in**
ordinary
**houses,
in**
ordinary
towns

yet
they
become

This book explains
how they achieve
that transformation.

1.YOU ARE WHAT YOU THINK YOU ARE

Creative people are not especially creative.

My work in the creative industries has introduced me to many great writers, artists and musicians. I have seen that they do not contain a bigger bank of creativity than anyone else.

The gift that creative people have is that they believe they are creative, and because they think they are creative, they are creative.

Many of these people lack traditional artistic abilities (Bacon couldn't draw, so he didn't; Warhol couldn't paint, so he didn't) but that doesn't stop them from thinking of themselves as creative.

The power of our minds is indisputable. Drug addicts take placebos and feel no withdrawal symptoms. Allergy sufferers sneeze at plastic flowers.

Hypnotised patients undergo surgery without anaesthesia. If the mind can alter the physical body, it can certainly alter the way we perceive ourselves.

Creative people live creative
lives because they think
of themselves as creative.

When Picasso was three or
four he was no more or less
creative than any other child.
The difference was that he
never stopped thinking of
himself as creative. He was
encouraged by his artist
father to believe that he was.

Whatever you think you are is
what you will be.

Successful creative people
like Beethoven, Picasso
and Dickens always thought
their work was great. Even
when they were young and
their work was in its infancy,
they had belief in themselves
that they were the best.

This self-belief accounts for
90 per cent of the reason why
they became the best.

"WE MUST HOLD ENOR- MOUS FAITH IN OURSELVES."

Giorgio de Chirico

2.

Inner belief and conviction creates resilience. Self-belief carries the creative through troubled times. It is a shield from the negativity of others.

The creative person's refusal to compromise can make them unpopular, but the important thing is to create at all costs.

Critics and the public attacked the early work of Édouard Manet. He painted ordinary working people with loose, sketchy brush strokes and simplified details, which was innovative and radical for the time. Manet's work was ridiculed when exhibited in private galleries. The Paris Salon consistently rejected his work.

When Manet wanted to exhibit at the Paris World's Fair, no one was interested. But he didn't adapt his work to make it more acceptable; he simply built his own pavilion and put on his own exhibition.

When his painting Olympia was finally accepted by the Salon, the public jeered and spat at it. Critics savaged it. Caricatures appeared in newspapers. He carried on regardless. His belief in himself was unshaken.

In later years Manet was vindicated when the Impressionists came to revere him as the pivotal figure in the transition from Realism to Impressionism, and he finally gained the recognition he deserved.

He didn't let the critics change his mind, he changed theirs.

'CONFIDENCE IS CONTAGIOUS

BUT SO IS LACK OF CONFIDENCE' Vince Lombardi

If you are an actor, produce a play and cast yourself.
If you're a writer, publish your own book.
If you're in a rock band, record and distribute your own CD.

You have to believe in yourself and your work. If you don't, how can you expect anyone else to?

There will always be tough times. There will always be critics. Something has to carry you through the difficult times. It can only be your inner belief in yourself. Happiness is not an absence of problems, but the determination to deal with them.

3. KEEP GOING...

To achieve anything worthwhile takes persistence.

It is a common belief that creativity is something you are born with and others can only envy. Wrong. Creativity is a skill that everyone can learn.

People understand that to become skilled at tennis or skiing you have to put in hours of practise. The same is true of creativity.

Often, ideas arrive in a flash of illumination, but they need to be refined, analysed and improved exhaustively.

The creative are persistent.

Ray Bradbury set himself the task of writing one short story every week. Ten years and 520 short stories later, he wrote one strong enough to publish.

Newton's idea that there was a force he later called gravity came to him in a flash when he saw an apple fall. He spent years developing and improving the theory.

Darwin conceived his theory of natural selection in a moment of inspiration. It took him twenty years to refine and finally publish it.

Alfred Butts invented the game Lexico when he became unemployed in the Great Depression. Players built words from nine tiles. Every game company rejected his concept.

Butts persisted. He continued to refine the game.

He added a board.
Again it was rejected.
He gave point values to each letter.
It was rejected.
He changed from nine tiles to seven.
It was rejected.
He added points to the squares on the board.
Again and again it was rejected.

He asked for advice and joined forces with James Brunot who changed the name to Scrabble. Eventually in 1952, after twenty years of trying, Macy's department store placed a huge order. Two years later, Butts had sold five million Scrabble sets.

To be creative you have to relentlessly develop and improve yourself and your ideas.

... EVEN WHEN YOU CAN'T

Successful creative people work wherever they are and however they feel. They don't wait for ideal conditions because they may never happen. The perfect workplace or mood does not exist.

The writer Jean Genet wrote novels when he was a convict in prison. He had nothing to write on so he used sackcloth and smuggled them out to be published.

When Henri Matisse was in his mid 70s and battling old age he became seriously ill and underwent surgery. Recuperating in France, he triumphed over his pain and disability and produced remarkable works of art.

Matisse needed a nursing assistant to keep him propped up with pillows to enable him to breathe. He was a painter, but he could not paint in bed, so he changed to collage, a medium that was new to him and began making collages with large sheets of paper that he cut with scissors and his nurse held up for him to see.

From his bed, despite the pain he was in, Matisse designed every single aspect of a chapel known as The Rosaire Chapel in Vence, France — the windows, crucifix, candlesticks, vestments, stained glass windows, and floor. This prodigious task was possibly his greatest achievement

Don't set up conditions — I can't work when I am tired, I need silence, I need my favourite pen, I can only work at night, I can't work because I've got a headache, I need music playing. Don't let anything stop you from creating, wherever you are, however you feel.

The creative never take a vacation.

5. LIVE THE DREAM

At school the word 'daydreamer' is an insult. A child who dreams and has their 'head in the clouds' is condemned as unrealistic and impractical. To allow the mind to wander off on fantastic adventures of its own making becomes something to be ashamed of.

Yet everything we are surrounded by — cars, clothes, furniture, houses — was first a dream in someone's head; a fantastic adventure experienced in the mind. They dreamt it, drew it, then created it. The practical minded miss the fact that we live in a world of dreams. Dreams that have been made tangible.

Paul McCartney dreamt the melody for 'Yesterday'. He composed it in a dream one night. Waking, he ran to a piano and played the tune to avoid forgetting it. McCartney wondered if he had subconsciously plagiarized someone else's work. For months he asked friends whether they had heard it before. Eventually, convinced that he had not stolen the melody, McCartney wrote lyrics and 'Yesterday' was born.

> YOU SEE THINGS; AND YOU SAY WHY?
> BUT I DREAM THINGS THAT NEVER WERE;
> AND I SAY WHY NOT?

George Bernard Shaw

The mind needs to meander and roam. With freedom it ends up in unusual places, creating new worlds, new ideas, new inventions.

Daydreamers created our television programmes, buildings, music, films and books.

WE LIVE IN THE DREAMER'S WORLD.
BE A CONTRIBUTOR,
NOT A DETRACTOR.

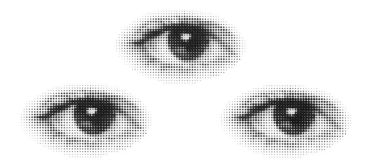

THE SLEEP OF REASON PRODUCES MONSTERS.

Francisco de Goya

6. STOP MAKING SENSE

In our life and work we often feel under pressure to do what is sensible.

To live a creative life you need to be liberated from being sensible. Enjoy doing something for the pleasure of doing it. Not because it is the logical or rational thing to do. The purpose of doing something is the pleasure you get from doing it.

A technique called 'Exquisite Corpse' was created by one of the Surrealists, André Breton, to liberate the mind from logic and connect to the inner wisdom of the subconscious. An image is collectively assembled by a number of people. A person draws on a sheet, folds the paper to conceal the image, then passes it to the next person who continues it without seeing what has gone before; and so on. Participants draw without knowing the direction in which the others may develop the image. They sketch anything that comes to mind, in a stream-of-consciousness way, whether trivial, perceptive or weird.Only at the end is the whole bizarre image revealed.

The Surrealists sought out the nonsensical and absurd because it liberated the mind from logic. Ideas and thoughts flowed freely.

THE PRESSURE TO BE SENSIBLE IS STIFLING AND SUFFOCATING.

7. THINK IN IMAGES

We live in a left-brain orientated society in which we are encouraged to think in words and numbers.

Researchers have proved that the more creative a person is, the more visually they think. The creative develop ways to block out verbal thoughts. They visualise ideas. They form mental pictures of their subject or problem. This enables them to see their idea.

Physicist Niels Bohr thought of the atom as a mini solar system, with electrons orbiting around a central nervous system.

The discovery by Frederich August Kekulé von Stradonitz of the fact that Benzine molecules were closed rings was a result of a dream in which he saw snakes swallowing their own tails.

Einstein stated that numbers and language played no part in his thought process. He created 'clear images which can be voluntarily reproduced or combined'.

> **IMAGINATION IS MORE IMPORTANT THAN KNOWLEDGE. KNOWLEDGE IS LIMITED. IMAGINATION ENCIRCLES THE WORLD.**

Albert Einstein

Einstein's discovery of the Special Theory of Relativity came about as the result of him imagining himself travelling at the speed of light and holding up a mirror. He tried to visualise what he would see in the mirror. Would the light from his face catch up to the mirror?

Language and numbers are linear. One word follows another, one sentence follows another and on and on. You are forced to think in a logical, linear way.

Visual thinking (right-brain thinking) is much more fluid and increases inspiration.

Whenever you are trying to think of ideas, concentrate on forming visual images in your mind.

Better still, draw them.

8. GIVE UP THE DAY JOB

Successful creative people dedicate themselves to what they care about most. They don't get a day job to pay the bills and reduce their real passion to a hobby.

When Caesar landed in Britain, the Roman troops disembarked. Then he burnt their boats. Without boats, they couldn't retreat. There was no safe way back. Everything became black and white. There was either success or death.

Don't give yourself the option of mediocrity and safety. If you have something to fall back on, chances are you will. Wasting your time and energy on something you don't care about will come to seem natural.

Under pressure from his family and banker father, Paul Cézanne was forced to study law at university. They believed it would lead to a safe and secure future. Cézanne felt crushed

> **ON THE RIDGE WHERE THE GREAT ARTIST MOVES FORWARD, EVERY STEP IS AN ADVENTURE, AN EXTREME RISK. IN THAT RISK, HOWEVER, AND ONLY THERE, LAYS THE FREEDOM OF ART.** Albert Camus

and squeezed between his family's ambitions for him and his real passion, art. He endured law school for two years where he felt squashed and repressed, then rebelled and left for Paris to become an artist. Cézanne's family was appalled at this recklessness and disowned him.

Cézanne changed the course of art history with his reduced, simplified shapes. Eventually, his family became reconciled and was proud of his achievements.

Whatever it is you most want to do: do it. If you try and fail, at least you've tried.

If you don't try you will always wonder what might have been.

Work for yourself, and then the power is in your own hands. If you work for someone else they can sack you. Most people stop working the moment they find a job. They sit back and coast.

Spending your life doing something you don't really care about is the scary option. Looking back and thinking, could have, might have, and should have is the saddest feeling of all.

LOOKING BACK

SHOULD

COULD HAVE

IS THE SADDEST

AND THINKING,

<u>HAVE,</u>

OR <u>MIGHT</u>
HAVE,

THING OF ALL.

9. CREATE MEANING NOT

PRODUCT

THE IDEA IS MORE IMPORTANT THAN THE OBJECT.

Damien Hirst

What is the meaning of your work? Creative people focus on the meaning of what they do. They ensure that what they do has significance for them and, therefore, for others. Their concern is to produce something worthwhile that has real human value. They care little for technique or slick effects.

The most viewed film of all time is Abraham Zapruder's footage of John F. Kennedy's assassination. It lasts only twenty seconds and can be seen as a catalogue of technical errors. There are camera shakes; the framing is poor – at the crucial moment, when a bullet strikes the president, the image nearly disappears from the bottom of the frame; the film constantly goes in and out of focus.

Despite a host of technical deficiencies, it is watched because of its strong, fascinating and compelling content.

The filming is rough and harsh. The mistakes even add to the atmosphere of the film – it's rawness and sense of immediacy. Ironically, it's technical inadequacies influenced directors such as Oliver Stone to use a rough-and-ready documentary style.

CONCERN YOURSELF WITH THE CONTENT AND NOT THE TECHNICALITIES.

10. CREATE YOURSELF

Creative people create themselves. The philosopher Michel Foucault observed that modern mans relationship with himself is to make himself into a work of art. The task of modern man is not to find his inner self, but to invent himself.

The German artist Joseph Beuys viewed his life as an artwork, as if it were a drawing or sculpture to be imaginatively developed. He asked himself who he wanted to be. He then set about turning himself into that person.

During World War II, Beuys was a rear gunner in a Stuka dive bomber. His plane was shot down on the Crimean Front and crashed. In Beuys' account, nomadic Tatar tribesmen rescued him and wrapped his injured body in animal fat, honey and felt, for their healing properties and warmth. They spent many weeks nursing him back to health. Beuys used the event to invent his artistic identity and justify his use of unconventional materials — fat, honey and felt.

In reality the Tatars did not rescue Beuys. He was quickly recovered by a German search unit and taken straight to a military hospital. Beuys' invented his own history. He created his own myth as if he were a work of art. He was not content with who he was. He strove to invent a better version of himself. For Beuys, creativity was a state of mind. He applied creativity to every task in his life, no matter how mundane. With every decision, action and thought, we create. Our life is our creation.

The relationship we have to ourselves should be creative. We should think of everything we do as an act of creativity.

Be your own work of art. Don't find yourself; invent yourself.

I THINK OF LIFE ITSELF NOW AS A WONDERFUL PLAY THAT I'VE WRITTEN FOR MYSELF, AND SO MY PURPOSE IS TO HAVE THE UTMOST FUN PLAYING MY PART.

Shirley MacLaine

11.
MAKE FAILURE A STEPPING STONE TO SUCCESS

Failure is a perception, not a fact.

Decide for yourself what you consider failure or success. Your opinion is something you can remain true to while the opinion of others oscillates.

Many creations that were considered a failure at the time of invention have since been reassessed as successes. Failure is a natural part of the creative process. Do not see failure as a sign of defeat, but one of many stepping-stones to success.

Your response to failure is the key. Creative thinkers can have their paintings criticised, their manuscripts rejected, or their music savaged without losing their tenacity. They accept failure as part of the refining process and learn from their errors.

Leonardo da Vinci is popularly regarded as the quintessential Renaissance man and an inspirational role model. Da Vinci produced only seventeen paintings, a number of which were incomplete. His notebooks contained amazing information, but he failed to organise or publish them during his lifetime as he intended. As a mathematician he left no significant input into the development of the theories of mathematics. As a musician he left no record of his music. As an architect, none of his extensive plans for buildings and bridges were built. As a sculptor, he has left no work. Many large scale projects such as *The Last Supper*, *The Battle of Anghiari,* and the twenty-four foot tall *Sforza Horse* were never completed. You judge him. Success or failure?

THE ONLY WORK OF ART WHICH SUCCEEDS IS THAT WHICH FAILS.

Jean Cocteau

It is possible to be paralysed by too many choices; too many possible directions.

Begin wherever you are and with anything you have to hand. No matter how uninspiring or ordinary it might seem.

Simple, familiar things are hidden to us. They are so ordinary to us, we don't even notice them.

Whatever you are surrounded by is your world. Your world is your subject matter. Seek out the extraordinary in the ordinary.

12. BEGIN ANYWHERE

David Hockney painted Typhoo Tea packets because that was what he drank everyday and they were lying around. Warhol painted Campbell's soup cans because he had it for lunch everyday. Henry Moore drew sheep because they were in the field outside his studio.

THE IMPORTANT THING IS SOMEHOW TO BEGIN.

Henry Moore

Michelangelo would be awestruck and fascinated by a plastic spoon; Caravaggio by a light bulb; Vermeer by a rubber duck.

You have to look at the familiar as if you have never seen it before. Make this your starting point.

No one can go back and make a brand new start, but anyone can start from now and make a brand new ending.

13. CREATE CHANCE, BECAUSE CHANCE CREATES

The creative mind seeks chance and accident while everyone else seeks control and order.

Control and predictability are the enemy of creativity.

Chance is a catalyst and vehicle for progress in unimagined ways. It is invigorating because it takes you down paths you didn't know existed.

Open yourself to what is unsure, uncertain and unstable.

The composer Amadeus Mozart sometimes used chance to compose music. He created a system that involved random lines of music and dice, in which he had to create music from disparate bars of music selected randomly using a chance throw of the dice.

Mozart was already extremely prolific and considered himself the greatest composer ever. So why did he want to bring chance into his method? Because he felt he was developing habits and repeating himself. Chance forced him to work in new and unexpected ways.

In the 1960s the modern composer John Cage took chance even further by creating a randomizer computer program to select unpredictable notes, random bars of music and how they should be played.

Build chance into your life and working method.

If you take chances you will lose your way occasionally. If you don't take chances you will certainly lose yourself.

14. CONTROL TECHNOLOGY

OR IT WILL CONTROL YOU

NO SENSIBLE DECISION CAN BE MADE ANY LONGER WITHOUT TAKING INTO
ACCOUNT NOT ONLY THE WORLD AS IT IS BUT ALSO THE WORLD AS IT WILL BE.

Isaac Asimov

Keep up to date with technology. It reshapes and restructures every aspect of our lives and our thinking. To live creatively, you have to be at the forefront of new developments, not lagging behind.

Technology defines us. It sets us apart from animals. A shovel made from antlers, the printing press, and the computer: they shaped our world and therefore our thoughts. We create technology but technology also creates us.

You will have yesterday's answers to today's questions if you don't keep up to speed with new technology.

The artist Umberto Boccioni was an Italian Futurist. He wanted to tear Italy from its Renaissance past into the dynamic reality of modern culture. Instead of resisting new inventions, Boccioni celebrated them.

His zest for the new and drive for progress was celebrated in his work. It exemplified the Futurist veneration for all that was new and dynamic. He worshiped the speed of modern life. His sculptures used the sleek polished metal that echoed the modern machinery. His work was a raucous celebration of technology.

Embrace new technology because it brings new ideas.

THE FUTURE IS HERE BUT YOU PROBABLY HAVEN'T NOTICED IT.

It's essential to be a technology gourmet. Don't be controlled by technology, pick what is useful to you. Don't allow technology to overwhelm you – learn to live with it well.

15. ONLY DO WHAT YOU ARE PASSIONATE ABOUT

If you are passionate about what you do, people will be drawn to you and your work. Your passion will spread to others. They will pay you for it.

Paradoxically, you will achieve more than those driven by worldly ambitions and goals.

If money is the goal, it is an empty ambition that everyone will see through.

Success is doing something as well as possible. It cannot be measured in cars or houses. Don't do anything for wealth or fame.

The creative don't suddenly change their lifestyle when they achieve success. They continue going to their studios and working exactly as they did before. When artists like Lucien Freud, Chaim Soutine and Georges Rouault achieved fame, they didn't buy Ferraris and holiday in Florida. They continued painting everyday, almost as if nothing had changed.

That is what they most wanted to do.

Do what you believe in and others will believe in it too. People will support someone with a passion. They will want to help you and money will be part of that help.

Be a magnet for money, don't let money be a magnet for you.

16. JOIN FORCES AND BE A FORCE

Many creative people link up
with someone who provides a
counter-balance to their talents.
If disorganised, they team up with
someone organised; if introverted,
they combine with an extrovert; if
emotional, they find someone rational.

Gilbert and George, Jagger and Richards, Gilbert and Sullivan,
Jake and Dinos Chapman achieved success because their talents
enhanced and amplified each other's.

The Beatles were greater than the sum of their individual parts.
Lennon and McCartney pooled their talents and their abilities
bounced off each other and multiplied. Whatever talent was lacking
in McCartney was counter balanced by a surplus in Lennon, and
vice versa. The Beatles work was essentially an argument between
Lennon and McCartney that was good to listen to.

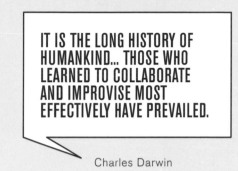

IT IS THE LONG HISTORY OF
HUMANKIND... THOSE WHO
LEARNED TO COLLABORATE
AND IMPROVISE MOST
EFFECTIVELY HAVE PREVAILED.

Charles Darwin

When they stopped working together it became apparent
that Lennon's work was harsh and lecturing without
McCartney's softening touch. McCartney's work was often
saccharine and sentimental without Lennon's harshness and
punch. But together, they added to each other. Working with
someone good made them each raise their standards, they
challenged each other. Their approaches were very different,
often antagonistic, rivals trying to out-do each other. It wasn't
an easy relationship, but it worked.

Having someone else to bounce ideas off can help the flow
of inspiration.

...AT THE BEGINNING

Play with the frameworks that surrounded you.

The creative mind plays with structures. It pulls things to pieces and puts them back together in new ways.

Every work needs structure. But the structure should be disorganised.

Contemporary architects play with expected formats of a building. A stable building is a safe structure, but boring.

An unstable building that looks as if it's about to fall over, like the Leaning Tower of Pisa, is disconcerting and, therefore, memorable and unique. Modern architects that have designed buildings to look as if they are about to fall over, have already collapsed, or moved.

Orson Welles

Jean-Luc Godard was one of cinema's great directors. His revolutionary films challenged audience's expectations. Godard relished subverting conventional structure. He wanted films to have a beginning, middle and end, but not necessarily in that order.

Goddard divided a film's structure into segments, with sections of narrative, long unbroken sequences of speech, long silences, characters that were the first to turn to the lens and address the audience directly, jump cuts, wobbly handheld shots and off-screen crashes. This kept the audience wondering what was coming next.

Take the structure of whatever you are working with, dismantle it and rearrange it. Jumbled up, it is likely to be more interesting.

17. PUT THE END...

18. QUESTION EVERYTHING, EVERYWHERE, FOREVER

Many problems arise from making assumptions. If you assume, you think you know when you probably don't.

Questioning destroys assumptions. Ask questions of yourself constantly. You can learn more by looking for an answer than finding it.

Questions are more important than answers because they help you to be more engaged with your subject.

Visitors to galleries spend an average of eight seconds looking at a painting. Amsterdam's Rijksmuseum restored Rembrandt's famous painting The Night Watch at great cost. To extend the time visitors spent observing the painting, the curators asked them to submit questions.

The curators selected the 50 most popular questions and supplied answers. Many questions focused on topics curators don't like to address: Can you prove Rembrandt painted it? How much is it worth? Are there any good forgeries of it? Are there mistakes in the painting? Why is it good?

These questions and answers were pinned near to the painting. The average viewing time increased to half an hour. Visitors alternated between reading questions and answers and examining the painting. They looked closer, for longer.

Questions stimulated curiosity. They raised awareness of the richness and complexity of the painting. Constantly challenge fundamental assumptions and preconceptions.

ANY QUESTIONS?

JUDGE A MAN BY HIS QUESTIONS RATHER THAN BY HIS ANSWERS.

Voltaire

MILLIONS
HAD SEEN AN
APPLE FALL.
NEWTON WAS
THE ONE WHO
ASKED WHY.

19. DON'T COMPETE

CREATE

> # THE ONLY COMPETITION WORTHY OF
> # A WISE MAN IS WITH HIMSELF.

Washington Allston

Don't enter awards or competitions. There can only be one winner. If there are 5000 entrants, it follows that there are 4999 losers. Do you want someone you have never met branding you a loser?

The internationally renowned artist Joseph Beuys was professor of sculpture at the prestigious Kunstakademie Düsseldorf. The selection procedure to this exclusive academy was rigorous and many applicants were rejected.

Beuys did away with the selection procedure and accepted anyone who applied. He felt unable to judge or select an applicant because he believed that creativity was the capacity of everyone, not a select few.

Accepting hundreds of applicants caused chaos, as the university could not cope with the huge increase in numbers. Beuys was dismissed from his post by less creative thinkers.

Work to the best of your ability. Judge Yourself.

20. BURST
THE *bubble*

Don't look for fashion in a clothes store or history in a museum.
Look for fashion in a grocers and history in a funfair.

Every field has it own perspective on the world. It is unusual
and surprising to step outside the bubble of your chosen field.

Investigate the latest developments in medicine, current
events, music, fashion, physics, horticulture, television, pig
farming, whatever.

Make sure you know what is new, what is changing, what is
coming next.

The key to Picasso's success was that he had an insatiable interest
in the world around him — science, music, literature — whatever.

View every subject as a potentially fertile source of inspiration.

Cubism was a movement developed by Picasso and Braque that changed the art world forever. They were inspired by science. Picasso attended a lecture on advanced mathematics. The lecturer showed new work about viewing complex Polyhedra in four dimensions. Multiple images of these objects were projected to show them in different perspectives at the same time.

Picasso wondered, why not paint multiple perspectives all at once? Cubism, the most significant art movement of all time, was born.

THE UNKNOWN WAS MY COMPASS.
THE UNKNOWN WAS MY ENCYCLOPEDIA.
THE UNNAMED WAS MY SCIENCE AND PROGRESS.

Anaïs Nin

21. BE PROUD TO BE DIFFERENT

Most people want to be accepted. They want to conform.
They want to do what everyone else does. Don't worry if
people think you and your methods are odd or unusual. It's
an advantage to be unique. Original thinkers don't automatically
adopt the practices of others in their field of work. They
develop their own working methods. This leads to different
ways of thinking.

Michael Faraday was a physicist who did not work within the
limits of the mathematics and science of the 19th century.
He had little formal schooling beyond primary level, yet he
discovered the induction of electricity, was one of the great
founders of modern physics and one of the most influential
scientists in history.

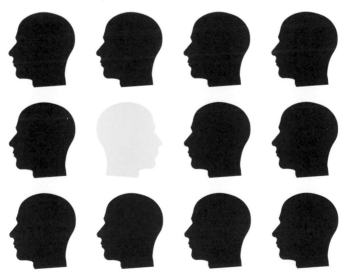

Most of Faraday's school hours were spent running wild in the streets. His ignorance of mathematics was directly responsible for his unique results. When investigating electrical and magnetic phenomena he had to develop his own non mathematical approaches. His lack of education was an attribute. It forced him to work in an independent and original way.

Education forces an individual to behave and think in the patterns society has dictated. Faraday was able to have a wider sense of awareness and question accepted practices while other scientists accepted the ground rules uncritically. He developed his own methods. Different methods led to different – and spectacular – results.

It's good to be different.

22. BE UNREASONABLE

Being reasonable and logical are not characteristics of successfully creative people.

Logic and reason cannot explain *Les Demoiselles d'Avignon*, *Sgt Pepper*, *Apocalypse Now* and *The Catcher in the Rye*. Picasso The Beatles, Francis Ford Coppola, and J. D. Salinger were fuelled by the desire to produce something startling, extraordinary and unique, not something practical and sensible.

The architect Gaudi designed the cathedral Sagada Familia in Barcelona. It is one of the great masterpieces of Western architecture. It has no parallels. The shape and scale are totally unique.

His vision produced something original, extraordinary elaborate and expressive. The project was so demanding he declined all other projects to devote himself to it. The Sagada Familia was so complex and intricate that Gaudi predicted it would take a further 200 years to finish. The excessive didn't daunt him. He prepared detailed plans and models for the project to be completed after his death.

Gaudi worked out what he wanted to do, then went ahead and did it. He didn't consider what others thought was reasonable. It made sense to him – if not to others. No one reasonable could have created the Sagada Familia.

It's OK to be unreasonable. To solve an exceptional problem, to get people to think in an entirely new way, or to crack an impossible task, you need someone driven not by logic but by emotion, passion and desire.

IF PEOPLE NEVER DID SILLY
THINGS, NOTHING INTELLIGENT
WOULD GET DONE.

Ludwig Wittgenstein

23. DON'T HURRY TIME

You must live at the speed that suits you. Don't force things.
To be truly creative you must work at your own pace.

If you work quickly, you work quickly. If you work slowly, you
work slowly.

Work at the speed that suits you and your project.

Throw away your watch. A project has its own time frame.
You may need to work day and night for weeks, or it may take
only a few minutes.

To be successful creatively, you have to ignore pressure and
work at the pace that suits you. Leonardo da Vinci took 25
years to complete *The Virgin of the Rocks*. Some of Picasso's
paintings took a few minutes. Vermeer produced only 35
paintings in his lifetime.

Warhol's assistants created several works a day for him. Edward
Hopper produced only two paintings a year. They were all
successful artists. They worked to the timeframe that suited
them.

Don't impose a time frame on yourself. Let your work tell you
how long it needs.

> ## THE HOLY GRAIL IS TO SPEND LESS TIME MAKING THE PICTURE THAN IT TAKES PEOPLE TO LOOK AT IT.
>
> Banksy

24. GO WITH THE FLOW GO WITH THE FLOW

Do not devise a plan and then slavishly
follow it. To live creatively you must go with
the flow and see what evolves.

Listen to the work you are producing and it will
tell you how it wants to progress.

The French Ministry of the Arts presented Rodin with a major
commission, the creation of a huge set of doors Rodin called
The Gates of Hell. Rodin was fired with enthusiasm and
produced many sketches and models of figures straining to
emerge from the substance of the door.

It inspired several iconic works. *The Thinker* originally jutted
from the top of the doorframe, but Rodin separated it.
It became a work in its own right. Detached, it became more
powerful. It depicts the monumental effort of artistic creation.
Similarly, *The Kiss* was removed from the door and took on an
independent life. As did *The Three Shades* and many others.

Rodin followed where the work led. He went with the flow and
allowed the project to dictate to him how it should progress.
He ignored the patron's deadlines and expectations. For years
the ministry officials pestered him for a completion date. Finally
they gave up. *The Gates of Hell* was never finished, but it
generated many masterpieces.

The creative are sensitive to the work and what it requires. They let the
project evolve naturally. The work knows best. Listen to its demands.

GO WITH THE FLOW GO WITH THE FLOW GO WITH THE FLOW

THE QUALITY OF THE
IMAGINATION IS TO FLOW
AND NOT TO FREEZE.

Ralph Waldo Emerson

I WORK WITH THINGS LEFT OVER FROM OTHER THINGS.

Julian Schnabel

To live creatively you have to avoid being predictable.
The creative mind seeks out unpredictable materials
because they lead to unpredictable ideas.

Don't buy your materials from the appropriate shop.

If you work in an office, don't buy your materials from office
supplies. If you work as an architect, don't use materials from
a builder's merchant. If you're gardener, don't use materials
from a garden centre.

If you are an artist, don't buy materials from an art-supplies
shop. Buy them from a chemist, a toyshop, a butcher's, a pet
shop, a garage or an electrical shop: anywhere other than
where you should buy materials.

25. USE THE WRONG TOOLS

Different materials will force you to do things differently.
That will force you to think differently.

The usual materials will lead you to work in the usual way.

Jenny Holzer is an artist who does not use traditional
materials. She uses words. Holzer is famous for her short
statements, called 'truisms', often phrases on random subjects
in the form of slogans.

Her medium is words. To convey them she uses LED signs,
plaques, benches or projections. They surprise people. The
signs do not convey the usual messages.

The materials we use lead us. It is a two-way process; we
control them but they control us. Unexpected materials will lead
you in unexpected directions.

26. DON'T STRIVE TO BE ORIGINAL

Many people give up because they feel they are not original or unique.

Don't make it your goal to be original. That is too high an aspiration, too difficult a starting point. Think of yourself as the next link in the chain of your chosen field. Simply try to nudge things forwards a little further.

That way, you are not measuring yourself against impossible standards but, in the long run, you might end up producing something original.

Many artists lean heavily on the work of others for support in the early stages. Later, they develop their own voice. If you set

out to copy a Turner, for instance, you will never be able to copy it exactly. It will always be slightly different. That difference is unique to you and will become greater. The more you work, the bigger that difference will become. That difference is what is unique and original about you.

Jackson Pollock's drip technique did not appear out of the blue. Max Ernst exerted a strong influence on young American artists in New York in the 1950s.

Ernst describes the way he instructed the young American painters on his oscillation technique: 'Tie an empty can to a piece of string one or two yards long and drill a small hole in its bottom. Now fill the can with paint and allow it to swing backwards and forwards over a flat canvas. In this way, amazing lines will trickle onto the canvas.' The method produced paintings identical to Jackson Pollock's. Pollock explored the technique and developed it to higher levels.

It is OK to use another's work as a starting point. You will enter into your work more and more and the other artist will leave.

Don't worry about being original. You are original. It's a matter of developing the confidence to be who you are.

DON'T WORRY

ABOUT YOUR

ORIGINALITY

IT WILL

REVEAL ITSELF NO

MATTER WHAT YOU OR

OTHERS DO.

27. DO WHAT YOU LIKE

Do what you like because
then you will like what you do.

The chances are that if you like what you do, others will too.

If you do something because you think it
is what you ought to do, or because it is the
clever or sensible thing to do, you will ultimately
lose interest and become dissatisfied. You'll turn
into a cog in someone else's machine.

Don't ask what the world needs. Ask what makes you feel
most alive. Then go and do it. What the world needs is people
who are feeling invigorated by life.

When the American artist Cindy Sherman was a child, her
favourite pastime was playing dress-up. She had a chest full
of dressing up clothes and enjoyed spending hours transforming
her appearance.

As an artist, Sherman did what she enjoyed most.
She continued role-playing. She dressed herself as a series of stereotypical characters familiar from popular culture such as secretaries, librarians and femme fatales, and photographed herself posing in appropriate settings. Her work was based on what she took pleasure in.

Do not be a solicitor by day and a surfer at the weekend. Be a surfer.

There is a perception in society that work is a chore that you must not enjoy. It is something to get through. We spend roughly fifty hours a week at, and travelling to and from, work. If it isn't rewarding, your life isn't rewarding.

What you do is who you are. Your work should touch your soul.

Don't let people make you feel bad about doing something you enjoy. They are the ones who are wasting their lives.

Whatever it is you most enjoy, make it the basis of your life and work. You will never lose interest in it.

28. DOES A FIVE-YEAR-OLD UNDERSTAND YOU?

It's possible to become lost in language and ideas. To use words to make yourself sound clever, rather than actually be clever.

Sum up what you are doing in a sentence.

If you explain your idea to a five-year-old and they don't understand it, there is something wrong with the idea.

Instead of shaving cream, Albert Einstein used hand soap for shaving. A friend once asked him why. His answer was 'Two soaps? That is too complicated.'

Einstein owned only one pair of shoes. The moment they wore out he bought a new pair and immediately threw out the old. Although trivial, these examples illustrate a process central to Einstein's thinking. Both in his work and life, he was compelled to simplify.

"BREVITY IS THE SISTER OF TALENT."

Anton Checkov

Einstein found existing equations about electricity and magnetism too complicated. Two different sets of equations were needed to describe a single principal.

In the introduction to the Theory of Relativity, Einstein explained that he was inspired to develop his new ideas because the existing ones were too awkward and ugly. The Theory of Relativity was born out of his desire to simplify. He summed up everything in one short equation.

People hide behind jargon. Complex language hides the lack of an interesting idea. They are saying look at how clever I am, not how clever the idea is.

Summing up your idea succinctly will help you to clarify what it is you are doing. There may be many deep and complex layers hidden within a work but Shakespeare's plays, Mozart's operas and Monet's water-lily paintings can each be summed up in a sentence or two.

SAY ONE THING AND SAY IT WELL

29. STOP. BEFORE.

At any stage, the innovative ask, can I stop at this point?

Obsessing over detail is stifling. Perfection is a work that is resolved, not one that is polished.

Michelangelo left four unfinished sculptures of slaves struggling to be free from their bonds. Unfinished, they were considered of little importance and languished in the vaults of the Louvre for years.

The slaves were an example of Michelangelo's idea of 'liberating the figure imprisoned in the marble'. The projecting limbs were finished while those further back were only rough-hewn. The slaves appear to be literally struggling to be free of the stone.

The unintentional pathos evoked by the unfinished figures had a huge impact on Rodin who saw in them an expressiveness that would be lost in a 'finished' work.

Influenced by Michelangelo's slaves, Rodin came to despise the appearance of 'finish'. He deliberately left work unfinished to leave something to the imagination of the viewer.

At the time the public's idea of perfection was a finished and polished sculpture. They considered Rodin lazy.

Rodin disregarded conventions and asserted that a work was finished when he had achieved his purpose.

> "PERHAPS THE SKETCH OF A WORK IS SO PLEASING BECAUSE EVERYONE CAN FINISH IT AS HE CHOOSES."
>
> Eugene Delacroix

THE. END.

30. DON'T SEE BARRIERS THAT AREN'T THERE

Many limitations and constraints are ones we have imagined for ourselves. Our thinking is inhibited because we unconsciously assume there are boundaries when there aren't any.

Don't work out what is possible. It is too limiting. If the correct course of action is impossible, set out to do the impossible. Decide on the correct course of action before you decide what's possible.

At a university I once taught a design class in place of an absent colleague. The students had been set a task to make a paper airplane from a single A4 sheet of paper that could travel 60 ft across the room. They generated a huge variety of designs but none could travel the distance. One student became so frustrated they scrunched up their paper airplane into a ball and threw it into a bin across the other side of the room.

When the students had all tried and failed, I took the scrunched-up paper out of the bin and declared it the winner. The students looked bewildered. I explained it was because it had travelled the required 60 ft.

WHO SAID AIRPLANES HAD TO LOOK LIKE AIRPLANES?

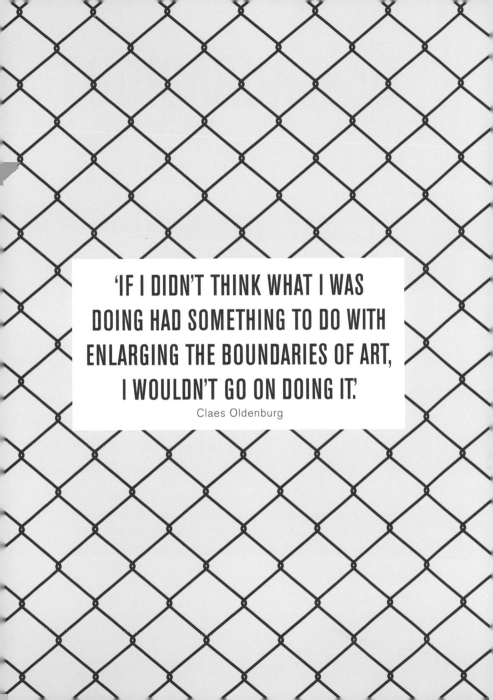

'IF I DIDN'T THINK WHAT I WAS DOING HAD SOMETHING TO DO WITH ENLARGING THE BOUNDARIES OF ART, I WOULDN'T GO ON DOING IT.'

Claes Oldenburg

31. BE AUDACIOUS

Audacity is essential to successful creativity. Unpublished novels lie in desk drawers, brilliant paintings are stacked behind wardrobes and gifted actors don't audition, all due to a lack of audacity.

It took audacity for Damien Hirst to put a shark in a tank of formaldehyde; for the Sex Pistols to stand onstage without being able to play their instruments; for Stanley Kubrick to rewrite the script of *The Shining* several times a day during shooting.

It took audacity for Marcel Duchamp to buy 'ready-made' mass-produced objects from a shop, then place them, unaltered on plinths in a gallery. The most infamous example is a urinal that he signed with the name of the manufacturer, R. Mutt. It caused a storm of controversy.

It took nerve to affront the art world with the ideas that technical skill was not essential and that an artwork does not need to be unique.

The successfully creative need the impudence required to put themselves forwards and be ridiculed. Often, they are as insecure and nervous as the next person, but they understand that no one can get things right all the time. Their confidence comes from not fearing to be wrong.

Many talented people fall by the wayside because of a lack of courage. Gifted people live in obscurity because of timidity. Creativity is not so much about talent as bravado.

FROM A REAL ANTAGONIST ONE GAINS BOUNDLESS COURAGE.

Franz Kafka

32. DON'T BE EMBARRASSED ABOUT MONEY

There is no point in pretending that money and creativity are separate. To live creatively you will have to deal with money, just as everyone else does.

Use the business side of creativity as a breather and rest.

A gallery is a shop. People walk in, like something, buy it and walk out with it. Everyone involved is embarrassed about that – the dealer, the artist and the collector. They avoid talking publicly about money. But that doesn't alter the fact that a gallery is a shop.

All the artists I've met who have had recognition and careers, have been good businessmen. They don't shout about it, but if they weren't they wouldn't remain artists.

Willem de Kooning and Jasper Johns shared the same dealer, Leo Castelli. De Kooning was annoyed with Castelli for some reason and said, 'That son-of-a-bitch; you could give him two beer cans and he'd sell them'. Jasper Johns heard this and thought, 'What a sculpture, two beer cans.' So Johns produced a sculpture of two beer cans and Castelli sold them.

Creativity is part of life and MONEY can't be

separated from life.

Don't pretend the link doesn't exist

– embrace it .

> WHY DO PEOPLE THINK
> ARTISTS ARE SPECIAL?
> IT'S JUST ANOTHER JOB.

Andy Warhol

33. BE AN EXTREMIST

How far can you take things? Be extreme, radical, intense and excessive. Whatever you are doing, push yourself and your work to the limit.

Examine every aspect of your life and work. Then push them as far forwards as possible. By going to extremes you break new ground.

Christo and Jeanne-Claude were partners that worked together as artists. They wrapped objects so that they were entirely obscured to the viewer. They made us curious about commonplace objects normally taken for granted.

In their early works they wrapped small objects such as bottles and magazines, then progressed to larger objects like motorcycles and shop fronts.

THERE IS NO SUCH THING AS EXAGGERATED ART. I EVEN BELIEVE THAT THERE IS SALVATION ONLY IN EXTREMES.

Paul Gaugin

Their works increased in scale and included the wrapping of the coast of Little Bay, Sydney, Australia, the Pont Neuf Bridge in Paris and the Reichstag in Berlin.

Christo and Jeanne-Claude's projects often received resistance from authorities and the public. When they set themselves the task of wrapping the Reichstag (the German parliament building), they had to work hard to convince the Members of Parliament, going from office to office, writing explanatory letters to each of the 662 delegates and making innumerable telephone calls and negotiations.

It took hundreds of assistants a week to wrap the building. 100 000 m² of fireproof polypropylene fabric, covered by an aluminum layer, and 15 km of rope were needed. Five million visitors saw the spectacle.

What can be exaggerated, overstated or understated? How would you approach your project if you had all the resources in the world, or no resources?

34. DON'T MAKE ASSUMPTIONS

To think creatively you must not be led by others. The creative take nothing for granted. If something is assumed to be true, they immediately question it. They find out for themselves.

Charles Darwin proposed the theory of evolution. He established that all species were descended over time from common ancestors. It was a dangerous idea that destroyed many deep beliefs. Darwin was rejected by medical school at Cambridge and showed a lack of interest in traditional learning. His failure at university meant he was free from established wisdom.

After traveling the world, Darwin sent thirteen birds from thirteen different islands, to the eminent zoologist John Gould for analysis. Gould was baffled; they were all finches, but slightly different. Scientific rules decreed that God had created a fixed number of unchanging species. Gould was the leader in the field. He had all the information in front of him but tried

IF WE ALL WORKED ON THE ASSUMPTION THAT WHAT IS ACCEPTED AS TRUE IS REALLY TRUE, THERE WOULD BE LITTLE HOPE OF ADVANCE.

Orville Wright

to fit it to the rules. He couldn't see that it was a perfect example of evolution.

Darwin wondered whether the finches were originally one species slowly evolving because of different environments. He didn't apply the rules so he was able to see evolution in front of him.

With less knowledge and expertise than other naturalists, Darwin changed the way we think. Darwin was the only naturalist not blinded by accepted knowledge. He didn't assume what he was being told was true. He worked things out for himself.

Don't make assumptions based on past knowledge. The creative mind does not assume something to be true until they have proved it themselves.

ASSUMPTIONS

SOON OUTLIVE THEIR USELESSNESS.

35. BE CRITICAL OF CRITICS

No one creative lives in a vacuum. Everyone needs feedback.

Not any feedback. You need someone whose judgement you trust. A collector may judge a work as to whether it fits with his existing collection; a gallery owner may judge it according to whether it will sell; a museum curator, according to whether it fits with current trends.

People will be critical of anything they don't understand. If you produce something new and unique, people won't know what to make of it. The public distrust anything new.

After the Beatles split up, one of the things that Paul McCartney found most difficult was getting honest criticism. The new musicians and producers he worked with were too respectful of McCartney to criticise anything he did. This was in stark contrast to John Lennon who had always been quick to point out weaknesses in his work.

ANYBODY WHO PAINTS AND SEES A SKY GREEN AND PASTURES BLUE OUGHT TO BE STERILIZED.

Adolf Hitler

Absorbing criticism can considerably advance your work. Don't ask for feedback because you need praise – use feedback to pinpoint the weaknesses in your work so they can be improved.

When someone looks at your work, they may not really be seeing or thinking about the work. They are probably thinking about themselves. They may be thinking, 'I don't want to upset this person so I'll be polite about this work' or 'I hate abstract art so I hate this work' or 'I want to say something that shows how clever I am.'

Parents, friends and colleagues can be savagely critical. It is often because they are venting their own frustrations and jealousies. Steer clear of them.

Choose your critic carefully. You need someone who can look at your work and judge it on its terms, not on his or her terms. You need an honest opinion, not an opinion.

36. KILL YOUR BABIES

The creative avoid wasting their time. If something isn't working out, they kill it off and start something new.

You become emotionally attached to a project you have invested a lot of effort in. It becomes precious. It becomes like a baby that you have nurtured.

But the more you try to save a project, the more overworked and laboured it becomes.

If you stop banging your head against a wall and move on to something more productive, you are exercising good judgement. It does not mean you have failed.

You are controlling the situation rather than letting it control you.

Francis Bacon was famous for destroying huge numbers of his paintings. He destroyed paintings he was dissatisfied with. Bacon was so ruthless that from the first fifteen years of his career only fourteen paintings survive. Even towards the end of his life the ritual slashing of rejected canvases with a knife continued. He would not let anything second rate leave his studio. Once, he was walking past a gallery when he saw one of his paintings in the window. He decided it wasn't as good as he once thought. He went into the gallery, bought the painting, took it outside and destroyed it.

He knew that the longer he worked on a painting, the more ponderous and turgid it would become.

Don't become locked into a project. If you fall in love with one idea, you won't see the merits of alternatives.

EVERY ACT OF CREATION IS
FIRST AN ACT OF DESTRUCTION.

Pablo Picasso

37.
BE
CERTAIN
OF

UNCERTAINTY

> CONSISTENCY IS CONTRARY TO NATURE, CONTRARY TO LIFE. THE ONLY COMPLETELY CONSISTENT PEOPLE ARE DEAD.

Aldous Huxley

Everything around you is constantly changing. Nothing is fixed. Nothing is forever. Successful creative people don't work against this knowledge but work with it.

Everything is in a state of flux. Boundaries between disciplines break down, values become increasingly blurred and change accelerates.

The Dada movement evolved in the financial and moral chaos of Western civilization after the First World War. Dada was a revolt against art by artists themselves.

Instead of attempting to make sense of the confusion or produce order from the chaos, Dada embraced it. They saw it as a release. They enjoyed it.

Dada's works reflected the flux and chaos they were surrounded by. They kept faith with absurdity and uncertainty. Their works lacked centre or focus.

The Dadaist Hans Arp threw a torn-up drawing onto the floor. He was struck by the new image created by the jumbled fragments arranged by chance. He stuck them down the way they had landed. He continued to work with cut up photographs and drawings to create a visual image of chaos.

A feature of contemporary culture is the speed of change and flexible values. Enjoy this uncertainty. Do not try to impose a false order.

Anyone who isn't confused doesn't truly understand what's going on.

38. TURN EVERYTHING on its HEAD

Successful creativity demands that we see something new.
Something in a way that others haven't.

Switching the mindset to think in opposites produces different
trains of thought that lead to different solutions.

The creative mind does the opposite of what is accepted.

It disrupts the standard way of approaching a subject and
searches for radical alternatives.

It is not searching for the right way or right answer, but for an alternative.

> I HAVE FORCED MYSELF TO CONTRADICT MYSELF IN
> ORDER TO AVOID CONFORMING TO MY OWN TASTE.

Marcel Duchamp

Doing the opposite of what is expected is a way of bringing about this change in perspective.

Hubert Cecil Booth invented the modern vacuum cleaner. In early design versions, the dust was blown into the air. This fitted with people's mindset of expunging dust. People were used to beating dust out of carpets and brushing it up from the floor.

Booth came up with the idea of sucking up the dust and equipped his cleaner with a filter, which kept the dust in the machine.

At first his invention was laughed at, but it slowly became accepted and appreciated.

The German painter Georg Baselitz achieved fame when he began to paint people and objects upside down. The inverted images force the viewer to reassess how they interpret the painting. Upended, the paintings lose most of their usual meaning and we cannot grasp them in the conventional way.

REVERSING YOUR PERSPECTIVE OPENS YOUR MIND AND LETS YOU VIEW YOUR WORK IN A NEW LIGHT.

When you are in the middle of a project, turn everything you are doing on its head.

Turn things inside out, make a small thing big, a big thing small, make something beautiful ugly and turn something black to white.

Whatever you are doing, ɹǝʌǝɹsǝ it.

OPPOSITE

TO BE DIFFERENT
AND HAVE SUCCESS
IN LIFE, YOU NEED
TO DO DIFFERENT
THINGS, TO DO THE
_____ OF EVERY-
ONE ELSE.

39. SIMPLIFY,

THEN SIMPLIFY MORE

Eliminate unnecessary details and distill down. Great creative minds keep things surprisingly simple.

Don't confuse simple with easy. It's easy to be complicated. It is difficult to subtract from your subject, spotlight and narrow down to the necessary.

In his exhibition *The New* Jeff Koons displayed brand new vacuum cleaners and carpet cleaners in Plexiglas containers lit by fluorescent lights. He did not alter the objects. The titles were simply the names of the objects, *New Hoover Deluxe Shampoo Polishers*, for example.

As art, these objects work on many levels – as symbols of desire and icons of the publics quest for order and cleanliness.

They remain eternally new, monuments to cleanliness.

If he had altered the objects he may have detracted from them. Koons allowed them to speak for themselves.

Details obstruct and confuse.

Can you state the narrowest definition of your subject?

What is the least you can do? What is unnecessary?

HOW DIFFICULT IT IS TO BE SIMPLE.

Vincent Van Gogh

40. FIND WHAT YOU'RE <u>NOT</u> LOOKING FOR

To live creatively you have to surround yourself with things that interest you. It's hard to be creative if you have got nothing to be creative with. If you start with nothing you have to invent everything from scratch.

The more information you gather, the greater the resources for the formation of new ideas.

Most creative thinkers are collectors, often of esoteric objects. The artist Joseph Cornell had an insatiable curiosity. He collected huge amounts of objects speculatively, anything he found interesting.

He was fascinated by discarded objects. On long walks through New York he scavenged for interesting ephemera in streets, junk shops and flea markets.

When he died his house contained 3000 books and magazines, thousands of records and films and tens of thousands of examples of ephemera filed into eccentric categories, such as spiders, moons, owl cut-outs, map tacks, watch parts and wooden balls.

His artwork consisted of glass-fronted boxes in which he arranged the objects. He constantly moved the contents, searching in his archive for the right combinations, continuously adding and removing, until the elements worked together. It took months for a satisfactory arrangement to appear.

The creative are curious, constantly on the lookout for the unusual. Their motives are not the monetary value but the intrinsic interest.

I THINK THE ARTIST HAS TO BE
SOMETHING LIKE A WHALE,
SWIMMING WITH ITS MOUTH OPEN,
ABSORBING EVERYTHING
UNTIL IT HAS WHAT IT NEEDS.

Romare Bearden

41. Be here, NOW

The successful creative mind focuses totally on the task at hand.

When daydreams, phone calls or emails disrupt your attention, you are prevented from concentrating fully.

You need to create a situation in which you have no choice other than to focus.

The 'white cube' of the gallery removes all distractions to enable you to focus on the work of art. Many artists replicate this in their studio.

René Descartes locked himself in a dark room for days, focusing on the question 'What is knowable?' and emerged with Rationalist Philosophy, an entirely new branch of thought.

Benny and Björn of the pop group Abba used to spend weeks locked away in an empty mountainside hut writing their music.

The American artist Tom Friedman had a typically messy studio. He became confused about his work and its direction.

He decided to empty his studio.

Nothing was left. No materials, chairs, equipment. Nothing.

He boarded up the windows and painted everything, including the floor, white. There were fluorescent light fixtures on the ceiling that cast a diffuse light so the edges of the walls were not visible.

Every day he brought an object into the studio and placed it on the floor. He spent all day examining and thinking about it, its history, manufacture and cultural meaning.

He began to subtly manipulate the objects. He had developed a process that he used from that point on.

Focus your attention into a single beam; don't let it be diffracted in a thousand directions.

> ## THE ONLY WAY I COULD WORK PROPERLY WAS BY USING THE ABSOLUTE MAXIMUM OF OBSERVATION AND CONCENTRATION THAT I COULD POSSIBLY MUSTER.
>
> Lucien Freud

IF YOU WERE GOING TO DIE SOON AND COULD ONLY DO ONE THING.

WHAT WOULD IT BE AND WHY ARE YOU WAITING?

42. CREATE YOUR

Create the right environment and you create the right state of mind.

A workplace should induce the right mood. An environment in which it is enjoyable to spend time makes it easier to produce creative work.

Musicians can't wait to get into Abbey Road Studios to work. It has a unique atmosphere. The sound has been compared to taking a bath in a tub of warm chocolate. Based in a converted Georgian house, the high ceiling provides 5 seconds of reverb. The special ambiance is also due to its history. Edward Elgar was the first to savor the special mood in the world's first commercial recording studio. Tens of rock groups, most famously, the Beatles, produced their finest work there. Abbey Road brings out the best in musicians. They don't want to leave. There are no outside distractions and so they become totally focused. At Abbey Road it's easy to lose track of your surroundings and explore all sorts of ideas and possibilities. It enables musicians to do what they want to do.

Everyone has emotional and mental responses to a place. If a workplace is pleasurable, it can spectacularly increase the quality of work. It doesn't have to be huge or luxurious. It's the atmosphere that counts. A writer may write best in a cellar on a rainy day.

By creating the background for your day, you can lessen any friction in the flow and produce better work in less time.

ENVIRONMENT

THE WHOLE STUDIO SEEMED TO BE BRISTLING WITH PICASSO'S. ALL THE BITS OF WOOD AND FRAMES HAD BECOME LIKE HIS PICTURES.

Vanessa Bell describing Picasso's studio

"THINGS WHICH MATTER MOST MUST NEVER BE AT THE MERCY OF THINGS WHICH MATTER LEAST."
Johann Wolfgang von Goethe

43. DO WHAT IS IMPORTANT, NOT WHAT IS URGENT

We all feel under pressure from the omnipresent media to reply to emails, to-do lists, phone calls, texts etc. and sacrifice what is really important. That pile of emails will always be there. Modern communications can be a vortex that we fall into and disappear. Carrying out chores will never create groundbreaking remarkable work.

Put your creative work first. Start the day with your personal work. That's when you feel energized and industrious. You owe it to yourself to make your creative development the top priority.

Amadeus Mozart always put his music first. He would compose anywhere – at mealtimes, while talking to friends or playing pool and, most famously, while his wife was giving birth in the next room. He wrote huge amounts of music. Although he died young, it would take over eight days to play all of his music, one piece after the next, without stopping. He put creativity first. Great people treat trifles as trifles and important matters as important.

Do not spend the best part of the day, when you are fresh, completing chores. When you turn to your serious work, your energy will have dropped and it'll be harder to focus.

It takes time to create something remarkable – a novel, a design, a painting, a revolutionary new company. It will never seem as urgent as the pestering electronic media we are swamped with. The thing that is most important is often the most quiet.

44. DON'T LEAVE IDEAS IN YOUR HEAD

Weak ink lasts longer than a strong memory. Inspiration fades quickly from the mind. The creative put ideas on paper the moment they have them.

Beethoven always carried books of music paper with him to jot down musical themes. His notebooks contained 'concept sketches'. There is a drawing or painting for almost every day of Van Gogh's life after he took up painting.

Leonardo da Vinci kept remarkable sketchbooks of inventions, ideas and observations. The organization is haphazard. The writing is rushed, with little punctuation. Yet they are revealing. We learn about his thinking through them. Because he suffered from Attention Deficit Disorder, the piecemeal format suited him.

His notebooks started out as a tool for him to improve the quality of his paintings. Leonardo studied anatomy, plants and rocks so that he could depict them more authentically in his paintings. They became a record of his life-long fascination with nature and his genius for invention.

Sketchbooks capture the energy and excitement of the original idea before it has been filtered through the rational mind. The first time an idea hits the page it is often as good as it's going to get.

Take a sketchbook everywhere you go. Become addicted to it. Think of it as an idea store that keeps your mind free of clutter. You can write or draw in any situation. The process allows you to be more firmly in the present. Become addicted to drawing.

It's not until you record your ideas that you realise how many good ideas you have.

AMATEURS LOOK FOR INSPIRATION; THE REST OF US JUST GET UP AND GO TO WORK.

Chuck Close

45. DON'T WAIT FOR INSPIRATION

No one wants to waste hours waiting for inspiration. Instead of killing time until inspiration arrives haphazardly, the creative have methods to summon it at will.

The creative find ways to put themselves in a frame of mind in which they can get the best out of themselves.

Ludwig van Beethoven poured ice water over his head before work. Van Gogh drank Absinthe. Steven Spielberg had many of his best ideas driving on the freeway. The philosopher Emmanuel Kant worked in bed at the same time every day, looking at a tower through an open window with his blankets arranged in a specific order. Rudyard Kipling would only write with obsidian black ink. Albert Einstein always had his best ideas in the shower in the morning. He even considered having a shower installed in his studio so that he could work in it.

These people used their own methods to create a mental state in which new ideas could flourish. These practical methods changed their mood and made them receptive to new avenues of thought. In this way, they connected to their deeper resources.

46.
DON'T BE LIMITED BY YOUR LIMITS

Everyone has limitations. Creative thinking can find a way around seemingly insurmountable obstacles. That 'way' can produce results that are not only successful but also original and remarkable.

Sometimes the problems we face can seem like the walls of a maze we are trapped in, but there is a way out if you try hard enough to find it.

Many musicians have overcome severe limitations. Bob Dylan had a terrible singing voice; so he gave his lyrics the power his voice lacked. Guitarist Jerry Garcia of The Grateful Dead lost half of his right middle finger in a wood-chopping accident. A fire left Jazz guitarist Django Reinhardt's left hand partially paralyzed. Black Sabbath's Tommy Iommi lost the ends of two fingers on his right hand in an industrial accident. He created prosthetic tips and went on to be one of the most celebrated rock guitarists of the 1970s. These people all developed new playing techniques to overcome their limitations. This resulted in a unique and distinctive sound that made each of them stand out from the crowd.

If a guitarist can overcome the loss of fingers, then we can overcome almost anything. A creative solution to a seemingly impossible limitation can force people into new and original areas of creativity.

FEET, WHAT DO I NEED YOU FOR WHEN I HAVE WINGS TO FLY?

Frida Kahlo

Successful creative people don't make excuses – 'It would cost too much'; 'there isn't enough time'; 'don't have the right equipment'. Their attitude is that if there is something they want to do, there is always a way, and they'll find it. They don't think of all the reasons why they can't do something, but think of why they can.

Stanley Kubric's advice to aspiring filmmakers was – to get hold of a camera and make a film, any film. He knew that you had to do it. Then learn through experience.

The American horror film *The Blair Witch Project* was made with a production budget of $20,000 and only four actors. The film went on to gross over $250 million.

The film relates the story of three student film-makers who hike into the Black Hills in Maryland to film a documentary about a local myth known as the Blair Witch, and they go missing. The film was presented as their documentary pieced together from their footage. The audience are told that the students were never found, but their camera was recovered. This storyline enabled all the film to be shot by the actors, thereby avoiding the need for high production costs. All lines were improvised and nearly all the events in the film were fed to the actors day by day.

The real-life film-makers didn't have a camera. Buying a high-quality camera would have made a big hole in their budget, so they bought one and returned it to the shop for a refund after filming was completed, making their budget even lower.

With little equipment or money they made their own feature film. They loved making movies, so they made one.

Any project will throw up problems. Creative thinking can overcome them.

47. DON'T EXCUSE EXCUSES

IF NECESSARY, I WOULD EVEN PAINT WITH MY BOTTOM.

Jean-Honoré Fragonard

48. DON'T POSTPONE THE *FUTURE*

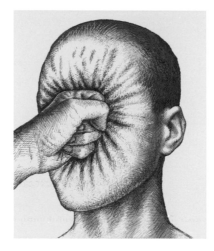

YOU CAN'T PUT OFF BEING YOUNG UNTIL YOU RETIRE.

Philip Larkin

Don't put off doing what is most important to you. Don't wait until you have enough money, enough time or the perfect home. Do it now, before it's too late.

Near-death experiences force people to re-evaluate their lives. The stark realisation of the possibility of death makes them want to get the most out of life. They make radical changes, switch to a more fulfilling job, move to the country, do the things they have always wanted to do but had put off. If only they could have made those decisions earlier.

The Russian writer Dostoyevsky was sentenced to execution with others considered to be subversives. His turn came and he stood before the firing squad. They presented arms. Ready. Aim. The order 'Fire' did not follow. An Imperial messenger had arrived just in time with a pardon from the Czar.

The trauma of facing the firing squad changed Dostoyevsky. He felt as if he had been granted a new life. He was energised. Dostoyevsky said it was like a punch in the face. It was his wake up call. He determined to devote himself to what was most important to him, writing. He underwent a deep spiritual transformation which led him to the conviction that redemption is only possible through suffering and faith. A belief that inspired his later acclaimed masterpieces, *Crime and Punishment*, *The Idiot* and *The Brothers Karamazov*.

Only postpone until tomorrow what you are prepared to die having left undone.

49. GO further THAN TOO FAR

We all have a comfort zone in which we feel safe.

Comfort is not stimulating but stifling.

Step outside and be challenged and inspired. Try to be adventurous every day and it will become second nature.

Only by risking going too far can you find out how far you can actually go. You can't learn to swim if you insist on keeping one foot on the ground.

Expanding your comfort zone creates confidence. If you are used to stretching your boundaries, when life throws up a shock, it won't have so much impact. You will be used to dealing with challenges.

The American artist Philip Guston achieved success as an Abstract Expressionist. Late in life he suddenly changed direction and started painting in a lugubrious cartoon style.

A giant leap in a different direction.

When Guston first exhibited his new figurative works they received scathing reviews. Critics could not accept that a painter they had for two decades counted as one of the heroes of Abstract Expressionism had, with no apparent warning, changed camps.

He is now best known for these cartoon-like paintings. Critics later revised their opinions.

ART IS AN ADVENTURE INTO AN UNKNOWN WORLD, WHICH CAN BE EXPLORED ONLY BY THOSE WILLING TO TAKE RISKS.

Mark Rothko

50. LEARN HOW TO LEARN

Those who have fresh, new ideas are always learning.

Learning is not about creating a store of knowledge. To learn, the mind has to be free to flit anywhere it chooses, like a bird. The mind cannot learn for a purpose. It has to explore in an open-ended way. The point of learning is growth, and a mind, unlike a body, can keep on growing until we die.

It is more important to learn than to know. Knowledge is different from learning. Knowledge is a stockpile. It's a static accumulation.

The English artist David Hockney has constantly explored and learned new media. Hockney's early paintings of swimming pools in Los Angeles were in acrylic, a new painting medium at the time. He worked with the new Polaroid cameras to produce photo collage's using many prints of a single subject to create a composite image. He drew with Quantel Paintbox, a computer program that allowed him to sketch directly onto the screen.

'I DON'T THINK MUCH OF A MAN WHO IS NOT WISER TODAY THAN HE WAS YESTERDAY.'
Abraham Lincoln

In his 70s he created hundreds of portraits, still lives and landscapes using the iPhone and iPad.

Hockney remained curious throughout his life, constantly learning and exploring new materials. He was always moving forwards, exploring new ground, continuously being reinvigorated.

To learn requires you to constantly explore new ideas and new media. It calls for sensitivity and awareness to your surroundings, not slavish memorisation of information. Learn how to learn and you've learnt enough.

51. USÉ ENVY AS MO- TIVA- TION

Have you ever looked at the work of others and thought 'I wish I'd done that?' Instead of smouldering with jealousy a creative thinker follows this with, 'now I'll try'.

Use that wish as a catalyst. If they could do it, then why not you?

When the young Francis Bacon visited a major Picasso retrospective in Paris, he was awestruck. He thought, 'I wish I'd done that.' So he took up painting and tried. Picasso inspired and motivated him. Bacon's response was not, 'I'm not good enough', or 'It's too risky,' but 'Why not have a go?'

Bacon's early works look like Picasso painted them. He was trying to get under his skin, to see through his eyes. He was trying to work out what it was about Picasso's thinking that he felt so instinctively drawn to. When copying Picasso's work there was a difference between the original and Bacon's copy that was recognizably his. The more he worked, the more his own voice emerged. When Bacon was awarded a major retrospective, Picasso

visited and was awestruck.
He could then see through
Bacon's eyes.

Now artists like Damien Hirst
look around a Bacon exhibition
and think 'I wish I'd done that.'

If there is something that makes
you think 'I wish I'd done that',
do it.

You can look on at others'
achievements enviously, or use
them as motivation. If they could
do it, so can you.

I don't like to think about being an influence. It's embarrassing.

Bruce Nauman

52. PLEASE YOURSELF, NOT OTHERS

Creativity flourishes when we remain true to our own values and ideas.

The Tatlin Tower was an imaginative groundbreaking building that soared diagonally 400 m into the St Petersburg sky. The architect Vladimir Tatlin created the radical modernist design in 1921 in response to a commission.

The visionary building had an iron spine that dramatically lurched from the ground at 60 degrees. A giant double-helix lattice of grey metal entwined it, shored up by vertical and diagonal struts that narrowed to an imprecise zenith. A gigantic glass cylinder orbited once a day within the cage, beaming out messages to the city. Below it a glass pyramid gyrated once a month and, lower, a cube, once a year.

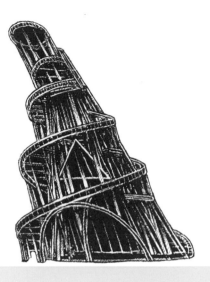

Well, not really. It was never built.

Tatlin was an artist who dared civic authorities to build a visual poem in iron. They didn't have the nerve. It doesn't exist, but that hasn't stopped it becoming one of the most iconic buildings of all time. The drawings and photographs of the model appear in hundreds of books on the history of architecture. Tatlin refused to design a traditional building the authorities would have approved of.

If commissioned to do work, keep faith with your own vision. If you try to please others, you may end up with something that doesn't please them or you.

Some people are good for you. They energise and enthuse you. Others are bad for you. They sap your power and drown you in negativity. High-achieving creative people have a way of surrounding themselves with the good and avoid the bad.

Many creative people are pulled down and destroyed by discouraging friends and family who want to lock them in a room marked 'dangerous'. They are persuaded that creativity is risky and perilous. They want to paint, write, perform or play music but are discouraged to take themselves seriously. They become afraid to pursue their dreams. Their promise goes unfulfilled.

The art critic Clement Greenberg championed the work of the unknown artist Jackson Pollock and encouraged him in every way possible. He persuaded collectors to buy his paintings, museums to buy and exhibit them, and wrote about Pollock in magazines and books. Greenberg energized Pollock with his enthusiasm for his paintings. He believed Pollock to be the

53. PLUG YOURSELF INTO AN ENERGY SUPPLY

ANYONE WHO EVER GAVE
YOU CONFIDENCE,
YOU OWE THEM A LOT.

Truman Capote

greatest painter of his generation. He argued that Pollock's
abstract canvases were the next stage in Modernist art; that
he was the true heir to Picasso and that Pollock's work had
advanced art to the highest, most advanced level possible. He
lifted Pollock's confidence to an incredible height.

A relationship is either nurturing or harmful. Some people can
suffocate you. Creatively frustrated people are like the
drowning; they try to drag others down with them. Creativity is
like oxygen and they are starved of it. It is painful for them to
see others expressing themselves.

Some people can make you feel energized and enlightened,
while others make you feel tired, drained or irritated. They are
toxic. Learn to identify them. Then keep away from them.

54.

RULE
YOUR
MIND
OR IT WILL RULE YOU

WITH SELF-DISCIPLINE MOST
ANYTHING IS POSSIBLE.

Theodore Roosevelt

Creativity requires an understanding of the difference between discipline and self-discipline.

Discipline is about self-denial and conformity to social or religious sanctions. External discipline uses rewards and punishments to regulate behaviour. It is restrictive and stifling.

Self-discipline is internal. It is shaped by inspiration, pride and satisfaction. It's unaffected by rewards or punishments.

The composer Irving Berlin set himself the task of writing one song every day, without fail. His songs left an indelible influence on the music of the 20th century. The first one to achieve worldwide success was 'Alexander's Ragtime Band' in 1911. Then followed 'White Christmas', 'Easter Parade', 'Puttin' On the Ritz', 'There's No Business Like Show Business' and more than 1500 songs.

How did Irving Berlin produce so much quality work? He must have been a genius? He didn't think so. He was humble when he explained how he wrote great tunes with memorable lyrics. He wrote an entire song, words, music, verse and chorus. Everyday. Many were poor quality and were discarded. But because he wrote so many, there were enough good ones to make him a success. His work was all about personal pride and meeting personal standards.

Discipline is essential, but it has to be self-discipline. Discipline must come from within rather than from without.

55. SET YOUR OWN STANDARDS

Aim to make whatever you are doing as good as humanly possible.

There are often pressures on us to compromise, to do the best under the circumstances.

Don't allow pressures to affect the quality of your work. Don't release anything second rate.

Determine what is for you, the best. Set your own standards of what you think you can achieve. Be your own judge.

The American artist Willem de Kooning set out to produce a painting that was as good as he could possibly create. The result was the iconic *Woman 1*, now an iconic artwork with a prominent place in art history.

He worked on *Woman 1* almost daily for two years. He would paint an image, feel dissatisfied, scrape it away and begin again. Every day he reconstructed the entire image. At least 200 individual versions were created on the canvas and subsequently destroyed. He was trying to find his own voice. He did not move on until he

found it. Eventually the painting reached a stage that de Kooning considered resolved. The painting appeared freshly made, as if completed in a single day.

He set himself a standard and did not accept anything that fell short.

Do not let the pressure of deadlines, finance, or other peoples' expectations force you to compromise. The creative are committed to their own standards. For the creative, work and play are seamless. They do not divide their life into earning money or spending it. Their reward is achieving inner standards of excellence.

56. TURN FEAR INTO FUEL

It's natural to feel apprehensive when embarking on a new venture.

A writer starts with a blank page, an artist, a blank canvas, and a composer, silence. Successful artists, musicians and writers don't have any less fear when staring into the unknown than anyone else.

What distinguishes them is that they engage their fear. They turn anxiety into energy. Action transforms their fear into vitality. Fear becomes fuel.

Many performers have battled with stage fright; Rod Stewart, Mel Gibson, Elvis Presley, Barbra Streisand, and Meryl Streep, to name a few. Many threw up, felt paralyzed or broke into cold sweats.

Laurence Olivier is often considered the greatest actor of the 20th century. He suffered from severe stage fright. It hit him hard and almost finished his career. When appearing at London's National Theatre, the stage manager had to push Olivier onstage every night.

THE DEMONS ARE INNUMERABLE, ARRIVE AT THE MOST INAPPROPRIATE TIMES, AND CREATE PANIC AND TERROR... BUT I HAVE LEARNED THAT IF I CAN MASTER THE NEGATIVE FORCES AND HARNESS THEM TO MY CHARIOT, THEN THEY CAN WORK TO MY ADVANTAGE...

Ingmar Bergman

Once on stage, Olivier, had no symptoms at all. Instead, he felt euphoria, similar to an athlete's rush of adrenaline. He played off the energy of his fear, using it to become more engaged in his performance.

It is hard for non-performers to comprehend why Olivier would put himself through such torment. He felt acting was what he was born to do. He felt fear because his performance meant so much to him. His love of acting overcame his fear.

All creative people feel dread and panic. The difference is that they feed off it. They turn it into a positive force.

57. MAKE IT HAPPEN

If you want something to happen, you will have to make it happen.

We find a million reasons to put off things. We talk, we plan and we procrastinate. Turning an idea into a reality takes effort. Only action will turn concepts into reality.

In 1988 I went to see an exhibition titled *Freeze* in London's Docklands. *Freeze* was where the young British artists including Damien Hirst and Gary Hume first burst onto the art-world stage.

Damien Hirst organised *Freeze* while still a student. It wasn't like most student exhibitions. Hirst stuck his neck out. He rented a huge warehouse. Such a huge exhibition was expensive, so he found sponsors. It mimicked the style and scale of the recently opened Saatchi Gallery. The exhibition and catalogue had unusually high professional production values. They were still students so the work was uneven, but the scale and ambition was impressive.

Hirst and his friends didn't go down the standard route of only putting up their work at their degree show in their university. They put on their own exhibition.

When I visited *Freeze* there was hardly anyone there. In truth, there were few visitors. It didn't matter. Hirst and his friends did enough to get noticed. It started a buzz. They were talked about and written about. Charles Saatchi purchased work. They had established a platform on which to build.

If you want to have an impact, you have to do something to get noticed.

While everyone else is thinking of reasons why a task is too difficult, impossible, the creative are thinking of reasons why it's possible.

A creative mind is proactive, not passive. Things happen around creative people.

ABOUT THE

AUTHOR

Rod Judkins is a fine-artist and lecturer based in London
He lectures in creative thinking at many colleges, including
Central St Martins. Since graduating from the Royal College
of Art he has had numerous solo art exhibitions in London
and abroad. This is his first book.

ACKNOWLEDGEMENTS

Thanks to Kate Pollard for believing in the book, Kajal Mistry for all her help, and Tom Skipp and Jim Green for their art direction.

Thanks also to Scarlet Judkins for being the model in the photograph in chapter 42 and Louis Judkins for being the model in the photograph in chapter 7.

ROD JUDKINS

Change Your Mind 2013 by Rod Judkins

First published in 2013 by Hardie Grant Books

Hardie Grant Books (UK)
Dudley House, North Suite
34–35 Southampton Street
London WC2E 7HF
www.hardiegrant.co.uk

Hardie Grant Books (Australia)
Ground Floor, Building 1
658 Church Street
Melbourne, VIC 3121
www.hardiegrant.com.au

British Library Cataloguing-in-Publication Data. A catalogue record
for this book is available from the British Library.

ISBN 978-1-74270-557-6

Illustrations on pages 14, 23, 24, 37, 38, 42, 50, 57, 63, 66, 68, 69, 74, 80, 89,
91, 106, 110, 112, 114, 116, 119, 121, 123, 125, 128, 131, 133, 134, and 135
© Rod Judkins.
All other images © iStockphoto LP 2010. All rights reserved.

Please visit www.rodjudkins.com

Commissioning Editor: Kate Pollard
Design concept by Tom Skipp

Printed and bound China by 1010 Printing International Limited

10 9 8 7 6 5 4 3